REAL CHANGE: CONVERSION

Bobby Jamieson
Mark Dever, General Editor
Jonathan Leeman, Managing Editor

HEALTHY CHURCH STUDY GUIDES

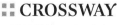

CROSSWAY

WHEATON, ILLINOIS

Crossway is a publishing ministry of Good News Publishers.

VP		22	21	20	19	18	17	16	15	14	13
15	14	13	12	11	10	9	8	7	6	5	4	3	2

"9Marks, as a ministry, has taken basic biblical teaching about the church and put it into the hands of pastors. Bobby, by way of these study guides, has taken this teaching and delivered it to the person in the pew. I am unaware of any other tool that so thoroughly and practically helps Christians understand God's plan for the local church. I can't wait to use these studies in my own congregation."

Jeramie Rinne, Senior Pastor, South Shore Baptist Church, Hingham, Massachusetts

"Bobby Jamieson has done local church pastors an incredible service by writing these study guides. Clear, biblical, and practical, they introduce the biblical basis for a healthy church. But more importantly, they challenge and equip church members to be part of the process of improving their own church's health. The studies work for individual, small group, and larger group settings. I have used them for the last year at my own church and appreciate how easy they are to adapt to my own setting. I don't know of anything else like them. Highly recommended!"

Michael Lawrence, Senior Pastor, Hinson Baptist Church, *Biblical Theology in the Life of the Church*

"This is a Bible study that is actually rooted in the Bible and involves actual study. In the 9Marks Healthy Church Study Guides series a new standard has been set for personal theological discovery and corresponding personal application. Rich exposition, compelling questions, and clear syntheses combine to give a guided tour of ecclesiology—the theology of the church. I know of no better curriculum for generating understanding of and involvement in the church than this. It will be a welcome resource in our church for years to come."

Rick Holland, Senior Pastor, Mission Road Bible Church, Prairie Village, Kansas

"In America today we have the largest churches in the history of our nation, but the least amount of impact for Christ's kingdom. Slick marketing and finely polished vision statements are a foundation of sand. The 9Marks Healthy Church Study Guides series is a refreshing departure from church-growth materials, towards an in-depth study of God's Word that will equip God's people with his vision for his Church. These study guides will lead local congregations to abandon secular methodologies for church growth and instead rely on Christ's principles for developing healthy, God-honoring assemblies."

Carl J. Broggi, Senior Pastor, Community Bible Church, Beaufort, South Carolina; President, Search the Scriptures Radio Ministry

"Anyone who loves Jesus will love what Jesus loves. The Bible clearly teaches that Jesus loves the church. He knows about and cares for individual churches and wants them to be spiritually healthy and vibrant. Not only has Jesus laid down his life for the church but he has also given many instructions in his Word regarding how churches are to live and function in the world. This series of Bible studies by 9Marks shows how Scripture teaches these things. Any Christian who works through this curriculum, preferably with other believers, will be helped to see in fresh ways the wisdom, love, and power of God in establishing the church on earth. These studies are biblical, practical, and accessible. I highly recommend this curriculum as a useful tool that will help any church embrace its calling to display the glory of God to a watching world."

Thomas Ascol, Senior Pastor, Grace Baptist Church of Cape Coral, Florida; Executive Director, Founders Ministries

9MARKS HEALTHY CHURCH STUDY GUIDES

CONTENTS

INTRODUCTION

What does the local church mean to you?

Maybe you love your church. You love the people. You love the preaching, the singing. You can't wait to show up on Sunday, and you cherish fellowship with other church members throughout the week.

Maybe the church is just a place you show up to a couple times a month. You sneak in late, duck out early.

We at 9Marks are convinced that the local church is God's plan for displaying his glory to the nations. And we want to help you catch and live out that vision, together with your whole church.

The 9Marks Healthy Church Study Guides are a series of six- or seven-week studies on each of the "nine marks of a healthy church" plus one introductory study. These nine marks are the core convictions of our ministry. To provide a quick introduction to them, we've included a chapter from Mark Dever's book *What Is a Healthy Church?* with each study. We don't claim that these nine marks are the most important things about the church or the only important things about the church. But we do believe that they are biblical and therefore are helpful for churches.

So, in these studies, we're going to work through the biblical foundations and practical applications of each one. The ten studies are:

- *Built upon the Rock: The Church* (the introductory study)
- *Hearing God's Word: Expositional Preaching*
- *The Whole Truth about God: Biblical Theology*
- *God's Good News: The Gospel*
- *Real Change: Conversion*
- *Reaching the Lost: Evangelism*
- *Committing to One Another: Church Membership*

- *Guarding One Another: Church Discipline*
- *Growing One Another: Discipleship in the Church*
- *Leading One Another: Church Leadership*

Each session of these studies takes a close look at one or more passages of Scripture and considers how it applies to the life of the whole church. So, we hope that these studies are equally appropriate for Sunday school, small groups, and other contexts where a group of anywhere from two to two-hundred people can come together and discuss God's Word.

These studies are mainly driven by observation, interpretation, and application questions, so get ready to speak up! We also hope that these studies provide opportunities for people to reflect together on their experiences in the church, whatever those experiences may be.

Do you think that people can change? I'm not talking about breaking a few bad habits or transforming from nerd to style icon. I mean real change. Change of the heart. Change of the whole person. Change that's deep and lasting.

In one sense, the Bible says that people cannot change. We are sinners by nature. Our hearts are corrupt and we can't make ourselves un-sinful, un-corrupt. Can a blind man make himself see? Can a dead man make himself alive? Those are the images Scripture uses to describe who we are by nature.

But that's not the whole story. The Bible tells us that God has the power to change. God can give sight to the blind. God can raise the dead. God can take out our hearts of stone and give us hearts of flesh. God can change us in ways that are deep and lasting.

The fundamental change the Bible talks about, and the change which sets in motion a whole life of Godward change, is conversion. Conversion is when God raises us from the dead, gives us eyes to see his glory, and grants us to turn from our sin and trust in Christ. Conversion may be a bad word to some in our culture, but it's a glorious, hope-giving biblical truth.

In this study we're going to look at the questions:

- Do we need to change?
- Is change possible?
- What is the change we need?
- How does this change happen?
- What are the fruits of this change?
- What does this change mean for the life of the church?

There is great hope in God's power to change. Let's explore that hope together.

AN IMPORTANT MARK OF A HEALTHY CHURCH: A BIBLICAL UNDERSTANDING OF CONVERSION

BY MARK DEVER

(Originally published as chapter 8 of What Is a Healthy Church?*)*

At my church's first meeting back in 1878, the church adopted a statement of faith. It was a strengthened version of the 1833 New Hampshire Confession of Faith. The old language may be a bit tough, but try to press through it. Article VIII of this statement reads,

> We believe that Repentance and Faith are sacred duties, and also inseparable graces, wrought in our souls by the regenerating Spirit of God; whereby being deeply convinced of our guilt, danger, and helplessness, and of the way of salvation by Christ, we turn to God with unfeigned contrition, confession, and supplication for mercy; at the same time heartily receiving the Lord Jesus Christ as our Prophet, Priest, and King, and relying on him alone as the only and all-sufficient Saviour.

Not many people speak or write like this anymore. Yet the biblical truths here haven't changed. A healthy church is marked by a biblical understanding of conversion.

OUR WORK
The statement begins with the biblical call to repentance and faith. As Jesus commanded at the beginning of his ministry, "Repent and

believe the good news!" (Mark 1:15 NIV). In the simplest terms, conversion equals repentance and faith.

As the confession continues, it provides a further description of what repentance and faith look like. It says we "turn" to God from our sin, we "receive" Christ, and we "rely" on him alone as the all-sufficient Savior. The New Testament is filled with pictures of sinners leaving their sin, receiving Christ, and relying upon him. Think of Levi the tax collector leaving his trade to follow Christ. Or the woman at the well. Or the Roman centurion. Or Peter, James, and John. Or Saul, the persecutor of Christians, turned Paul, the Apostle to the Gentiles. The list is long. Each of them turns, trusts, and follows. That's conversion.

It's not reciting a creed. It's not saying a prayer. It's not a conversation. It's not becoming a Westerner. It's not reaching a certain age, attending a class, or passing through some other rite of adulthood. It's not a journey, everyone strewn along the path at different points. Rather, conversion is turning with our whole lives from self-justification to Christ's justification, from self-rule to God's rule, from idol worship to God worship.

CONVERSION IS GOD'S WORK IN US

Yet notice what this statement also says about our conversion. We turn because we are "deeply convinced of our guilt, danger and helplessness, and of the way of salvation by Christ." How does this happen? Who convinces us? It is "wrought in our souls by the regenerating Spirit of God." The statement cites two Scriptures to support this idea:

> When they heard this, they had no further objections and praised God, saying, "So then, even to Gentiles God has granted repentance that leads to life." (Acts 11:18 NIV)

> It is by grace you have been saved, through faith—and this not from yourselves, it is the gift of God. (Eph. 2:8 NIV)

If we understand our conversion as something we have done, apart from what God first does in us, then we misunderstand it.

Conversion certainly includes our action, as we've discussed. Yet conversion is much more than that. Scripture teaches that we must have our hearts replaced, our minds transformed, and our spirits given life. We can't do any of this. The change every human needs is so radical, so much at our very root, that only God can do it. He created us the first time. So he must make us new creations. He was responsible for our natural birth. So he must give us a new birth. We need God to convert us.

The nineteenth-century preacher Roland Hill once told a story of how a drunken man came up to him and said, "I am one of your converts, Mr. Hill." "I daresay you are," replied that shrewd and sensible preacher; "but you are none of the Lord's, or you would not be drunk."

BAD FRUIT AND GOOD

When a church misunderstands the Bible's teaching on conversion, it may well become filled with people who made sincere pronouncements at one point in their lives but who have not experienced the radical change the Bible presents as conversion.

True conversion may or may not involve an emotionally heated experience. However, it will evidence itself in its fruit. Do lives give evidence of change—putting off the old and putting on the new? Are members interested in waging war against their sin, even if they continue to stumble? Do they show a new interest in enjoying fellowship with Christians and perhaps new motives in spending time with non-Christians? Are they beginning to respond to trials and challenges differently from how they did as non-Christians?

A right understanding of conversion will show up not only in the sermons, but in a church's requirements for baptism and the Lord's Supper. Care will be exercised. Pastors will not be pressured to baptize people hastily and without examination.

It will show up in the church's expectations for membership. Admittance is not immediate. Perhaps a membership class is offered. A testimony is requested, as well as an explanation of the gospel from the prospective member.

It will show up in the church's unwillingness to view known sin lightly. Accountability, encouragement, and the occasional rebuke are ordinary, not extraordinary. Church discipline is practiced.

Understanding the Bible's presentation of conversion is one of the important marks of a healthy church.

WEEK 1
DO WE NEED TO CHANGE?

GETTING STARTED

I like to think that I'm open to criticism, but when my wife actually offers some constructive feedback I get defensive and touchy. What's going on here?

1. It seems that many people get offended if someone even suggests that they need to change. What are some reasons why people get offended at this?

2. Do you get upset when someone suggests you need to change? If so, why? What does that show about your heart?

MAIN IDEA

All people desperately need to change because by nature we are alienated from God, rebellious toward God, and subject to the wrath of God.

DIGGING IN

Regardless of the fact that many people would oppose this idea, the Bible teaches that all human beings are in need of fundamental change.

Consider what Paul says about humanity in Romans chapter 1:

> [18] For the wrath of God is revealed from heaven against all ungodliness and unrighteousness of men, who by their unrighteousness suppress the truth. [19] For what can be known about God is plain to them, because God has shown it to them. [20] For his invisible attributes, namely, his eternal power and divine nature, have been clearly perceived, ever since the creation of the world, in the things that have been made. So they are without excuse. [21] For although they knew God, they did not honor him as God or give thanks to him, but they

became futile in their thinking, and their foolish hearts were darkened. [22] Claiming to be wise, they became fools, [23] and exchanged the glory of the immortal God for images resembling mortal man and birds and animals and creeping things.

[24] Therefore God gave them up in the lusts of their hearts to impurity, to the dishonoring of their bodies among themselves, [25] because they exchanged the truth about God for a lie and worshiped and served the creature rather than the Creator, who is blessed forever! Amen.

[26] For this reason God gave them up to dishonorable passions. For their women exchanged natural relations for those that are contrary to nature; [27] and the men likewise gave up natural relations with women and were consumed with passion for one another, men committing shameless acts with men and receiving in themselves the due penalty for their error.

[28] And since they did not see fit to acknowledge God, God gave them up to a debased mind to do what ought not to be done. [29] They were filled with all manner of unrighteousness, evil, covetousness, malice. They are full of envy, murder, strife, deceit, maliciousness. They are gossips, [30] slanderers, haters of God, insolent, haughty, boastful, inventors of evil, disobedient to parents, [31] foolish, faithless, heartless, ruthless. [32] Though they know God's righteous decree that those who practice such things deserve to die, they not only do them but give approval to those who practice them. (1:18–32)

1. Who is Paul talking about in these verses? every body

2. What are all the things that Paul says people do in this passage? List them all below. Does anything Paul says strike you, surprise you, or raise questions for you?

3. What is God's attitude toward humanity as described in this passage?
god gave them up
the wrath of god

4. What does Paul say can be known about God (vv. 19–20)? How are these things made known (v. 20)?
Creative things

5. How should we respond to this knowledge (v. 21)?
honor god,
give thanks, worship the creator

6. What have people done to the truth about God (See vv. 18, 21, 22, 23)?
suppress the truth, foolish hearts, rejecting the truth
exchange the truth refusing the truth

16

7. What has happened to our minds and hearts as a result? (See v. 28.)
heart become , futile, darkened, foolish, debased

8. How would you summarize this passage's teaching about human nature and God's attitude toward humanity as a whole? *, God will give you up.*

9. In light of this passage, how would you respond to someone who said that human beings are fundamentally good? *mind corrupt*

10. What evidence do you see in the world that this passage's teaching is true?

11. Why do you think it's important for us as Christians to clearly proclaim that people are in need of radical change? What would happen if we muted this part of the Christian message?

12. What are some ways that the local church as a whole can clearly communicate this need for change?

As Christians, we rejoice that this bad news about humanity is not the end of the story. We know that because God is good, he will punish sin. This is a fearful prospect since, as we've seen, all humans are rebels against God. Yet we also know that because God is merciful, he sent Jesus Christ into the world to live the perfectly obedient life that we should have lived and to die on the cross as a substitute for the sins of all who would ever trust in him. On the cross, God poured out his wrath against sin *onto Jesus*—not for any sin that Jesus had committed, but for our sins. And after three days Jesus rose from the grave, conquering death and vindicating his claim to be Lord and Savior.

And now God calls all people everywhere to the most radical, fundamental change possible: to repent of our sins and trust in Christ in order to be forgiven, accepted by God, reconciled to him, and given eternal life in fellowship with him.

The bad news is, we are in desperate need of change. The good news is that through Christ's death and resurrection, the change we need is possible. Our sinful natures can be renewed in God's image by the Holy Spirit, and we can be reconciled to God through Christ.

In the following studies we're going to consider more about how God changes us through the gospel, beginning with the fact that through Christ, the change we need is *possible*.

WEEK 2
IS CHANGE POSSIBLE?

GETTING STARTED

Many people today believe that people can't really change. We may be able to make some minor adjustments here and there, but we can't fundamentally change who we are.

1. What are some reasons why people believe this?

2. Do you think that people can really change? Why or why not?

MAIN IDEA

By God's grace, through the gospel, we *can* change. Through faith in Christ, by the power of the Holy Spirit, we receive a new nature that delights to do God's will.

DIGGING IN

In Acts 9 we read of the radical change God brought about in the life of Saul of Tarsus, who is primarily known to us as the apostle Paul.

> [1] But Saul, still breathing threats and murder against the disciples of the Lord, went to the high priest [2] and asked him for letters to the synagogues at Damascus, so that if he found any belonging to the Way, men or women, he might bring them bound to Jerusalem. [3] Now as he went on his way, he approached Damascus, and suddenly a light from heaven shone around him. [4] And falling to the ground he heard a voice saying to him, "Saul, Saul, why are you persecuting me?" [5] And he said, "Who are you, Lord?" And he said, "I am Jesus, whom you are persecuting. [6] But rise and enter the city, and you will be told what you are to do." [7] The men who were traveling with him stood speechless, hearing the voice but seeing no one. [8] Saul rose from the ground, and although his eyes were opened, he saw noth-

ing. So they led him by the hand and brought him into Damascus. [9] And for three days he was without sight, and neither ate nor drank.

[10] Now there was a disciple at Damascus named Ananias. The Lord said to him in a vision, "Ananias." And he said, "Here I am, Lord." [11] And the Lord said to him, "Rise and go to the street called Straight, and at the house of Judas look for a man of Tarsus named Saul, for behold, he is praying, [12] and he has seen in a vision a man named Ananias come in and lay his hands on him so that he might regain his sight." [13] But Ananias answered, "Lord, I have heard from many about this man, how much evil he has done to your saints at Jerusalem. [14] And here he has authority from the chief priests to bind all who call on your name." [15] But the Lord said to him, "Go, for he is a chosen instrument of mine to carry my name before the Gentiles and kings and the children of Israel. [16] For I will show him how much he must suffer for the sake of my name." [17] So Ananias departed and entered the house. And laying his hands on him he said, "Brother Saul, the Lord Jesus who appeared to you on the road by which you came has sent me so that you may regain your sight and be filled with the Holy Spirit." [18] And immediately something like scales fell from his eyes, and he regained his sight. Then he rose and was baptized; [19] and taking food, he was strengthened.

For some days he was with the disciples at Damascus. [20] And immediately he proclaimed Jesus in the synagogues, saying, "He is the Son of God." [21] And all who heard him were amazed and said, "Is not this the man who made havoc in Jerusalem of those who called upon this name? And has he not come here for this purpose, to bring them bound before the chief priests?" [22] But Saul increased all the more in strength, and confounded the Jews who lived in Damascus by proving that Jesus was the Christ. (Acts 9:1–22)

1. *What is Saul doing at the beginning of this passage (vv. 1–2)?*

2. *What happened to Saul as he was approaching Damascus (vv. 3–9)?*

3. *How does Ananias initially respond when the Lord Jesus tells him to go lay hands on Saul? What does this say about Saul's reputation (vv. 10–14)?*

4. *Describe how Saul's life changed immediately after his conversion (vv. 19–22).*

5. How did Paul's understanding of Jesus change as a result of this encounter? What did he believe about Jesus before and after this decisive meeting? (See vv. 20–22.)

6. How is Saul's conversion similar to all other Christians' conversions?

God's initiated Saul's conversion.

Obviously not all conversions are dramatic and instantaneous like Paul's. Some people come to Christ gradually, over a long time. And some people can't pinpoint the exact time of their conversion. That's okay. The Holy Spirit works in wonderfully diverse ways.

7. What are some other ways Paul's conversion might be different from other Christians' conversions?

In 1 Timothy 1, the apostle Paul reflects back on the great change God worked in his life, which began with the event we just considered:

> [12] I thank him who has given me strength, Christ Jesus our Lord, because he judged me faithful, appointing me to his service, [13] though formerly I was a blasphemer, persecutor, and insolent opponent. But I received mercy because I had acted ignorantly in unbelief, [14] and the grace of our Lord overflowed for me with the faith and love that are in Christ Jesus. [15] The saying is trustworthy and deserving of full acceptance, that Christ Jesus came into the world to save sinners, of whom I am the foremost. [16] But I received mercy for this reason, that in me, as the foremost, Jesus Christ might display his perfect patience as an example to those who were to believe in him for eternal life. [17] To the King of ages, immortal, invisible, the only God, be honor and glory forever and ever. Amen. (1 Tim. 1:12–17)

8. What are the different ways Paul describes himself (whether at present or in the past) in this passage?

9. What did Paul receive from Christ (v. 13)?

10. What is the "trustworthy saying" Paul gives us? What does this saying deserve (v. 15)?

11. For what purpose did Paul receive mercy (v. 16)?

12. What does it mean that Paul is an example of those who were to believe in Christ (v. 16)? What does this teach us about the possibility of real change through the gospel?

In case you're tempted to think that change only happens to apostles, consider what Paul says in 1 Corinthians 6:9–11:

> [9] Or do you not know that the unrighteous will not inherit the kingdom of God? Do not be deceived: neither the sexually immoral, nor idolaters, nor adulterers, nor men who practice homosexuality, [10] nor thieves, nor the greedy, nor drunkards, nor revilers, nor swindlers will inherit the kingdom of God. [11] And such were some of you. But you were washed, you were sanctified, you were justified in the name of the Lord Jesus Christ and by the Spirit of our God.

13. What does Paul say that some of us were?

14. What does Paul say has happened to us? How have we been changed?

Washed, sanctified, justified.

15. In light of all three of these passages, how would you respond to someone who said that people can't really change?

We are not bound to our sin
new life under holy spirit, permanent change

16. How should this good news that we can change in the most fundamental way through the gospel impact:

    a) Our prayers for our own lives?
    b) Our prayers for others?
    c) Our evangelism? brings change
    d) How we handle conflict in the church?
    e) How we interact with difficult or immature church members?

WEEK 3
WHAT IS THE CHANGE
WE NEED? *Spiritual / born again*
regeneration

GETTING STARTED

1. What are some things people commonly admit that they should change? What are some things people may be unwilling to admit that they should change?

2. In what ways do you think you should change? Why?

MAIN IDEA

Jesus teaches that in order to enter God's kingdom, we must be born again. God himself must give us a new nature in order that we would believe in Christ and do God's will.

DIGGING IN

In John 3, Jesus confronts Nicodemus with his need for radical change that can only come from God. We read,

> ¹ Now there was a man of the Pharisees named Nicodemus, a ruler of the Jews. ² This man came to Jesus by night and said to him, "Rabbi, we know that you are a teacher come from God, for no one can do these signs that you do unless God is with him." ³ Jesus answered him, "Truly, truly, I say to you, unless one is born again he cannot see the kingdom of God." ⁴ Nicodemus said to him, "How can a man be born when he is old? Can he enter a second time into his mother's womb and be born?" ⁵ Jesus answered, "Truly, truly, I say to you, unless one is born of water and the Spirit, he cannot enter the kingdom of God. ⁶ That which is born of the flesh is flesh, and that which is born of the Spirit is spirit. ⁷ Do not marvel that I said to you, 'You must be born again.' ⁸ The wind blows where it wishes, and you

hear its sound, but you do not know where it comes from or where it goes. So it is with everyone who is born of the Spirit."

[9] Nicodemus said to him, "How can these things be?" [10] Jesus answered him, "Are you the teacher of Israel and yet you do not understand these things? [11] Truly, truly, I say to you, we speak of what we know, and bear witness to what we have seen, but you do not receive our testimony. [12] If I have told you earthly things and you do not believe, how can you believe if I tell you heavenly things? [13] No one has ascended into heaven except he who descended from heaven, the Son of Man. [14] And as Moses lifted up the serpent in the wilderness, so must the Son of Man be lifted up, [15] that whoever believes in him may have eternal life." (John 3:1–15)

1. What does Nicodemus say about who Jesus is? How does he know (v. 2)?

2. What does Jesus say to Nicodemus in response (v. 3)? Why do you think Jesus says this? Need to be born again via spirit & water.

3. Does Nicodemus understand what Jesus means (v. 4)?

In Ezekiel 36:24–28, God promises his people that one day,

[24] I will take you from the nations and gather you from all the countries and bring you into your own land. [25] I will sprinkle clean water on you, and you shall be clean from all your uncleannesses, and from all your idols I will cleanse you. [26] And I will give you a new heart, and a new spirit I will put within you. And I will remove the heart of stone from your flesh and give you a heart of flesh. [27] And I will put my Spirit within you, and cause you to walk in my statutes and be careful to obey my rules. [28] You shall dwell in the land that I gave to your fathers, and you shall be my people, and I will be your God.

4. With this in mind, what do you think Jesus means when he says, "Unless one is born of water and the Spirit, he cannot enter the kingdom of God" (v. 5)?

5. Read verses 7 and 8. In what way are people born of the Spirit like the wind and its effects? What is the point of Jesus's comparison?
- dont know the spirit is coming
- cant see the " but you will see effect of the holy spirit.
- god chooses, god chooses where he goes

6. *Does Nicodemus understand what Jesus is talking about in verses 7 and 8?* He understand but how could it be possible.

7. *What does Jesus say about Nicodemus's failure to understand (vv. 10–13)?*
Man knows earthly things, but don't know heavenly things.

8. *What does Jesus say must happen to himself? What will be the result (vv. 14–15)?* Talking about the crucifixion

9. *Considering the passage as a whole, how would you summarize the change that Jesus says must happen in someone's life in order for them to enter the kingdom of God?* — Holy spirit come into your life.
— Must be born again, cleanse with your sin.

10. *How does this change come about? Is it something that we can bring about of our own power? (See also John 1:12–13.)* We don't have the power.
Being born when Jesus change you. God controls

11. *What are some common objections to the belief that you must be born again in order to enter God's kingdom? How would you respond to them biblically?*
— We want grace (grace undeserved gift.)
— No one is righteous.

12. *How should the reality that we must be born again in order to enter the kingdom of God impact:*

   a) Our prayers for others?
   b) Our evangelism?
   c) Any notion that we can win God's favor with our morality or good works?
   d) How we relate to those who claim to be Christians but whose lives don't match up to that claim?

WEEK 4
HOW DOES THIS CHANGE HAPPEN?

GETTING STARTED

1. Have you ever experienced a surprising, unexpected change in your life? How did it come about?

In the past few studies we've been considering conversion, the radical change that comes about when a person turns from their sin and trusts in Christ. In this study we're going to focus on how conversion happens.

MAIN IDEA

Through the gospel, by the power of the Holy Spirit, God gives new life to spiritually dead sinners. Conversion happens when God grants us a new nature and supernaturally enables us to repent of our sins and believe the gospel. *God initiates the change.*

DIGGING IN

In 1 Peter 1, Peter exhorts us to live lives that are marked by holiness and reverence toward God because God has saved us and given us an eternal hope. In verses 22 through 25 he writes,

> [22] Having purified your souls by your obedience to the truth for a sincere brotherly love, love one another earnestly from a pure heart, [23] since you have been born again, not of perishable seed but of imperishable, through the living and abiding word of God; [24] for
>
> "All flesh is like grass
>   and all its glory like the flower of grass.

> The grass withers,
> > and the flower falls,
> > 25 but the word of the Lord remains forever."

And this word is the good news that was preached to you. (1:22–25)

1. What does Peter exhort us to do in this passage (v. 22)?

2. On what basis does Peter exhort us to love each other (vv. 22–23)?
- being born again
- abiding with truth

imperishable
seed = Christ

3. By what means have we been born again (v. 23)?
- by the living word of god, spiritually
- obedience, change our heart

4. What does it mean that the Word of God is "imperishable" seed (v. 23)? What does this teach us about the life we obtain through the new birth?
- imperishable - means word of god, no corruption
  eternal, true word. SEEDS = seed of the
  word is

5. What is the "word of the Lord" that gives us the new birth (v. 25)?
- the gospel   CHRIST.

In Ephesians 2, Paul writes about the radical change that took place in each of our lives when we came to Christ.

> 1 And you were dead in the trespasses and sins 2 in which you once walked, following the course of this world, following the prince of the power of the air, the spirit that is now at work in the sons of disobedience—3 among whom we all once lived in the passions of our flesh, carrying out the desires of the body and the mind, and were by nature children of wrath, like the rest of mankind. 4 But God, being rich in mercy, because of the great love with which he loved us, 5 even when we were dead in our trespasses, made us alive together with Christ—by grace you have been saved—6 and raised us up with him and seated us with him in the heavenly places in Christ Jesus, 7 so that in the coming ages he might show the immeasurable riches of his grace in kindness toward us in Christ Jesus. 8 For by grace you have been saved through faith. And this is not your own doing; it is the gift of God, 9 not a result of works, so that no one may boast. 10 For we are his workmanship, created in Christ Jesus for good works, which God prepared beforehand, that we should walk in them. (2:1–10)

6. How does Paul describe our spiritual state before our conversion (vv. 1–3)?
- dead
- course of the world

28 - passion of the flesh
   - children of wrath

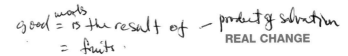

good words = is the result of — product of salvation
= fruits

7. What happened to us to bring about such radical change (vv. 4–5)?

— god raised from spiritually dead

8. Why did God save us, give us new life, and raise us up with Christ (v. 4)? What does this teach us about God's character? *because of mercy and love.*
   — fellow believers
   — loving god, he takes the initiative, we deserve death
   — compassionate, holy,

9. What are the results of conversion that this passage describes (vv. 5–10)?
   — united in christ | *— walking w/christ* | *— eternity*
   — make us alive w/christ | *— kindness* | *— workmanship*
   — raised up | *— immeasurable riches* |

10. What role do our good works play in salvation (vv. 8–10)?
    — no role

From both of these passages we learn that through the gospel, by the power of the Holy Spirit, God gives new life to spiritually dead sinners. Conversion happens when God grants us a new nature and enables us to repent of our sins and believe the gospel. This conversion comes not as a result of our good works but by God's sheer grace. And it gives us a new life, a new hope, and a new ability to live a life that pleases God.

11. Why do you think it's important for a local church to clearly teach about how conversion happens? What will be some results of good or bad teaching on this topic? *— No confusion, no false message*

12. Churches can affirm the doctrine of conversion, but then effectively rely on worldly devices to bring people to Christ instead of the Word and Spirit. What are some of the things we, as churches, can wrongly rely upon to "make the difference" in people's lives?

13. What are some ways that reflecting on our spiritual death and the new life God has sovereignly given should impact:

   a) How we handle sin in our lives?
   b) How we respond to criticism?
   c) Our prayers for others?
   d) Our relationships in the church?

WEEK 5
WHAT ARE THE FRUITS OF
THIS CHANGE? (PART 1)

GETTING STARTED

1. *Have you ever known someone who claimed to be a Christian but whose life clearly didn't match what he or she professed to believe? How did you interact with that person?*

2. *What changes have come about in your life since you became a Christian?*

MAIN IDEA

Those who are truly converted are no longer enslaved to sin and no longer live in sin. Instead, they increasingly grow in loving God and loving others. In other words, the fruit of conversion is freedom from the habitual practice of sin.

DIGGING IN

In 1 John 3, the apostle John writes,

> [1] See what kind of love the Father has given to us, that we should be called children of God; and so we are. The reason why the world does not know us is that it did not know him. [2] Beloved, we are God's children now, and what we will be has not yet appeared; but we know that when he appears we shall be like him, because we shall see him as he is. [3] And everyone who thus hopes in him purifies himself as he is pure.
>
> [4] Everyone who makes a practice of sinning also practices lawlessness; sin is lawlessness. [5] You know that he appeared in order to take away sins, and in him there is no sin. [6] No one who abides in him keeps on sinning; no one who keeps on sinning has either seen him or known him. [7] Little children, let no one deceive you. Whoever

practices righteousness is righteous, as he is righteous. [8] Whoever makes a practice of sinning is of the devil, for the devil has been sinning from the beginning. The reason the Son of God appeared was to destroy the works of the devil. [9] No one born of God makes a practice of sinning, for God's seed abides in him, and he cannot keep on sinning because he has been born of God. [10] By this it is evident who are the children of God, and who are the children of the devil: whoever does not practice righteousness is not of God, nor is the one who does not love his brother. (1 John 3:1–10)

children of god . Children of the devil.

1. What has God made us in Christ? What does this show us about God (vv. 1–2)?
make us his children. love, merciful, father,

2. What does John mean when he says that "what we will be has not yet appeared" (v. 2)? *Not like Jesus.*

3. What does "everyone who thus hopes in him" do (v. 3)? Why? What does this look like practically? Give specific examples. *purifies himself, not practice sin. Obey, pray, love each other.*

4. Why did Jesus "appear," that is, come to earth (vv. 5, 8)?
take away sin.
destroy the work of the devil.

5. According to John, people who habitually practice sin:

   a) Also practice ___lawlessness___ (v. 4).
   b) Have neither ___seen___ nor ___known___ Jesus (v. 6).
   c) Are of ___the devil___ (v. 8).
   d) Are not ___of God___ (v. 10).

How would you summarize John's teaching about those who consistently live in sin? Are such people born again? _ *No*

6. Why do you think John warns his readers, "Little children, let no one deceive you. Whoever practices righteousness is righteous, as he is righteous" (v. 7)?

7. According to John, everyone who is truly born again:

   a) ___Purifies___ himself (v. 3).
   b) Doesn't ___keep on sinning___ (v. 6).

32

c) Practices _righteousness_ (v. 7).
d) Does not and cannot _make_ a _practice_ of sinning (v. 9).

How would you summarize John's teaching about those who have truly been born again?

8. Why is it that no one who is born of God makes a practice of sinning (v. 9)? What does this mean? new birth, regeneration.

9. Is John teaching that Christians are perfect and never sin? (See 1 John 1:8–9; 2:1–2.) No,

As we've seen, conversion is demonstrated by its fruits. Those who are truly converted will live lives that are marked by righteous obedience to God's commands, rather than a habitual practice of sin.
regeneration —> fruit

10. What are some ways that churches obscure or contradict this truth in their:

   a) Preaching?
   b) Practice of church membership?
   c) Practice of baptism and the Lord's Supper?
   d) Small groups and other contexts for fellowship?

11. What are some ways that churches can display and recognize this truth in their:

   a) Preaching?
   b) Practice of church membership?
   c) Practice of baptism and the Lord's Supper?
   d) Small groups and other contexts for fellowship?

12. In his book Finally Alive, *John Piper has written about the temptation Christians have to slide into either presumption or despair.*

When we slide into presumption, we grow lukewarm and careless about the Christian life, even using God's grace as an excuse to justify our sin.
   When we slide into despair, we sink down in fear and discouragement because we are more aware of our ongoing struggles with

sin than we are of God's gracious work for us and in us. Our conscience condemns us because even our good deeds seem so imperfect that they couldn't possibly prove that we're born again.[1]

a) How would you apply the truths of 1 John 3:1–10 to someone who was sliding into presumption?

b) How would you apply the truths of 1 John 1:8–9 and 1 John 2:1–2 to someone who was sliding into despair?

---

[1]John Piper, *Finally Alive* (Fearns, UK: Christian Focus, 2009), 149–50.

WEEK 6
WHAT ARE THE FRUITS OF
THIS CHANGE? (PART 2)

GETTING STARTED
1. How would you feel if someone claimed to love you but they clearly hated your family? What's wrong with that picture?

In this session we're going to see that those who truly love God also love God's people. Our love for fellow Christians is one of the fruits of conversion. And it's one of the ways we can tell whether we have been converted.

MAIN IDEA
Those who are converted will love their fellow Christians, which proves their love for God.

DIGGING IN
In our previous study, we learned from 1 John 3:1–10 that all those who have been born again are freed from the habitual practice of sin and will lead righteous lives that please God. In this study, we're going to examine 1 John 4:7–21, which fleshes out what those righteous lives are to look like:

> [7] Beloved, let us love one another, for love is from God, and whoever loves has been born of God and knows God. [8] Anyone who does not love does not know God, because God is love. [9] In this the love of God was made manifest among us, that God sent his only Son into the world, so that we might live through him. [10] In this is love, not that we have loved God but that he loved us and sent his Son to be the propitiation for our sins. [11] Beloved, if God so loved us, we also ought to

love one another. [12] No one has ever seen God; if we love one another, God abides in us and his love is perfected in us.

[13] By this we know that we abide in him and he in us, because he has given us of his Spirit. [14] And we have seen and testify that the Father has sent his Son to be the Savior of the world. [15] Whoever confesses that Jesus is the Son of God, God abides in him, and he in God. [16] So we have come to know and to believe the love that God has for us. God is love, and whoever abides in love abides in God, and God abides in him. [17] By this is love perfected with us, so that we may have confidence for the day of judgment, because as he is so also are we in this world. [18] There is no fear in love, but perfect love casts out fear. For fear has to do with punishment, and whoever fears has not been perfected in love. [19] We love because he first loved us. [20] If anyone says, "I love God," and hates his brother, he is a liar; for he who does not love his brother whom he has seen cannot love God whom he has not seen. [21] And this commandment we have from him: whoever loves God must also love his brother. (4:7–21)

1. Read through the whole passage and list everything that John commands us to do. What pattern do you see? What does this show us?

2. What does John say is true of those who love one another (vv. 7, 12, 16)?

3. What does John say about those who do not love others (vv. 8, 20)?

4. How has God shown his love for us (vv. 9–10, 14–16)?

5. What reasons does John give for why we should love one another (vv. 7, 11, 19, 21)?

6. What are the results of our faithfully loving one another (vv. 12–13, 16, 17–18)?

7. Based on the teaching of this passage, can someone truly love God if they don't love their fellow Christians (vv. 20-21)?

As we've seen in this passage, John teaches that the fruit of genuine conversion is love for God and love for others. Remember that, just as we saw in our previous study, this doesn't mean that we love each other perfectly (1 John 1:8–9; 2:2), though all genuine Christians will love their brothers and sisters in Christ. In fact, our love for fellow Christians is what proves that we really do love God.

Earlier in his epistle, John gives two examples of what this love looks like, of *how* we are to love one another. In 1 John 3:11–15, John writes,

> [11] For this is the message that you have heard from the beginning, that we should love one another. [12] We should not be like Cain, who was of the evil one and murdered his brother. And why did he murder him? Because his own deeds were evil and his brother's righteous. [13] Do not be surprised, brothers, that the world hates you. [14] We know that we have passed out of death into life, because we love the brothers. Whoever does not love abides in death. [15] Everyone who hates his brother is a murderer, and you know that no murderer has eternal life abiding in him.

8. Why did Cain kill Abel (v. 12)? What does this teach us about how sin responds to someone else's righteousness?

9. Cain killed his brother because his brother's righteous life exposed his unrighteousness. Rather than rejoicing in his brother's goodness, he attacked it. What does this passage's negative example of Cain teach us about how we should love one another?

In 1 John 3:16–18 we read more about how Christians are to practically love one another:

> [16] By this we know love, that he laid down his life for us, and we ought to lay down our lives for the brothers. [17] But if anyone has the world's goods and sees his brother in need, yet closes his heart against him, how does God's love abide in him? [18] Little children, let us not love in word or talk but in deed and in truth.

10. What does John say that we ought to do for our brothers (that is, fellow Christians)? Why (v. 16)?

11. How does John say we are to love one another (v. 18)? What test of our love does he give (v. 17)?

12. What are some ways that you have:

- a) Struggled to love others?
- b) Been loved by fellow Christians?
- c) Grown in laying down your life for fellow Christians?

13. Church membership should be a venue in which we live out this "deed and truth" kind of love for our brothers and sisters.

- a) What are some of the difficulties you face in loving your fellow church members in deed and truth? How do you work through them?
- b) What are some ways that being a member of a church has helped you to love fellow Christians in deed and truth?
- c) What are some practical ways you can grow in loving your fellow church members?
- d) Think about church members who have particular needs, such as widows. What are some practical ways to care for widows? Why is "deed-and-truth love" especially important in caring for widows and other particularly vulnerable church members?

WEEK 7
CONVERSION AND THE
CHURCH

GETTING STARTED

1. Has anything in our study of conversion in these past few classes surprised you? If so, what? Why?

2. Can you think of any reasons why conversion is important not just for individual Christians, but also for local churches?

MAIN IDEA

All those who are converted—and only those who are converted—should join a local church. When the church is filled with Christians, the Holy Spirit will fill the church with the fruit of spiritual growth, genuine fellowship, and more.

DIGGING IN

In this study we're going to draw from all we've learned about conversion in the previous studies and see how conversion impacts the church. In order to do that, we're going to look at the portrait of the earliest church which Luke gives us in Acts 2.

On the day of Pentecost, the Holy Spirit descended on the apostles and caused them to speak in tongues. In the midst of this, Peter stood up and proclaimed the meaning of these events, culminating with his explanation of the death and resurrection of Jesus. Let's pick up the story with his hearers' response in verse 37:

> [37] Now when they heard this they were cut to the heart, and said to Peter and the rest of the apostles, "Brothers, what shall we do?" [38] And Peter said to them, "Repent and be baptized every one of you in the

name of Jesus Christ for the forgiveness of your sins, and you will receive the gift of the Holy Spirit. [39] For the promise is for you and for your children and for all who are far off, everyone whom the Lord our God calls to himself." [40] And with many other words he bore witness and continued to exhort them, saying, "Save yourselves from this crooked generation." [41] So those who received his word were baptized, and there were added that day about three thousand souls.

[42] And they devoted themselves to the apostles' teaching and the fellowship, to the breaking of bread and the prayers. [43] And awe came upon every soul, and many wonders and signs were being done through the apostles. [44] And all who believed were together and had all things in common. [45] And they were selling their possessions and belongings and distributing the proceeds to all, as any had need. [46] And day by day, attending the temple together and breaking bread in their homes, they received their food with glad and generous hearts, [47] praising God and having favor with all the people. And the Lord added to their number day by day those who were being saved. (Acts 2:37–47)

1. What did Peter's hearers experience at the conclusion of his address? How did they respond (v. 37)?

2. What did Peter tell his hearers to do? (vv. 38, 40; see also v. 41)

As we've just seen, Peter urged his hearers to repent, be baptized, and save themselves from "this crooked generation."

- **Repentance** is turning away from sin and to God. It is changing the entire stance of one's life from self-rule to God's rule.
- **Baptism** is a public identification with Jesus Christ in his death, burial, and resurrection, and as such is a public profession of faith in him. Baptism also identifies one with God's people, the church, and functions as a pledge to live in the fellowship of the church.
- Finally, by "save yourselves from this crooked generation" Peter means that those who hear him must trust in Christ in order to be delivered from God's wrath, and they must also lead new and holy lives that are distinct from the world around them.

3. Who does Peter say that God's promise of forgiveness is for (v. 39)? What does this teach us about conversion?

4. What does it mean that "there were added that day about three thousand souls" (v. 41)? What were the three thousand added to?

5. What did these new believers devote themselves to as a church (v. 42)?

6. What did the new believers do with their possessions (vv. 44–45)? What does this teach us about their attitude toward one another? (Think back to our study of 1 John 3:16–18 from last time.)

7. What did the believers do "day by day" (vv. 46–47a)?

8. What did the Lord do to the church day by day (v. 47b)? What does this teach us about how the believers related to those outside the church?

As we've seen, this passage gives us a snapshot of conversion and what conversion means for the church. We see that:

- All those who were converted were added to the church.
- *Only* those who were converted were added to the church.
- All those who belonged to the church devoted themselves to the apostles' teaching, to caring for the needs of the saints, to regular corporate worship and fellowship, and to evangelism.

9. What do you think would have happened to the church in Acts 2 if, instead of being filled with genuinely converted Christians, it was filled with an even mix of genuine Christians and false professors? What do you think that would have done to their:

- Devotion to the apostles' teaching?
- Generosity with their possessions?
- House-to-house fellowship?
- Evangelistic efforts?

10. What are some ways that churches today might unwittingly allow unconverted persons into their membership?

11. What are some ways that churches can help ensure that:

    a) Those who join the church are truly converted?
    b) All those who are converted join and plant their lives in a local church?

12. How does this overall picture of life in the early church encourage and inspire you? What aspects of this picture are missing from your experience of the church? How could you go about cultivating them?

TEACHER'S NOTES FOR WEEK 1

DIGGING IN

1. In these verses Paul is talking about all of humanity. He says in verse 18 that the wrath of God is revealed against "men," and his descriptions seem to include all people in their sweep.

2. Regarding the more personal part of this question, answers will vary.

3. God's attitude toward humanity is wrath (v. 18). God is described as giving people over to their sin (vv. 24, 26, 28), indicating that in his wrath God is allowing people to sink deeper into sin.

4. Paul says that God's eternal power and divine nature can be known by all because they are clearly revealed in what God has made (vv. 19–20).

5. We should respond to this knowledge by honoring God (v. 21), giving thanks to him (v. 21), and worshiping and serving him (v. 25). In other words, we should respond to God's revelation of himself in creation by orienting our whole lives around him, obeying him in all things, and worshiping and submitting to him as Lord.

6. People have suppressed the truth about God (v. 18), refused to act in accord with it (v. 21), become fools by rejecting it (v. 22), and exchanged it for idolatry, which is a lie (v. 23).

7. As a result of exchanging the truth about God for a lie, our thinking has become futile and foolish (vv. 21–22) and our hearts have been darkened (v. 21). Paul also says that our minds have become "debased" (v. 28) because we have rejected the knowledge of God.

8. A basic summary of this passage would be that humanity is universally sinful, thoroughly corrupted by sin in mind and heart, is in a state of rebellion against God, and God is therefore wrathful toward humanity.

9. Answers will vary, but the basic idea is that the Bible teaches that human beings, far from being fundamentally good, are by nature thoroughly corrupt in our minds, hearts, wills, and actions.

10–12. Answers will vary.

TEACHER'S NOTES FOR WEEK 2

DIGGING IN

1. At the beginning of this passage, Saul is breathing out murderous threats against the disciples and traveling to Damascus for the specific purpose of persecuting Christians (vv. 1–2).

2. As Saul was approaching Damascus, Jesus appeared to him and said, "Why are you persecuting me?" and Saul fell to the ground and became blind.

3. Ananias initially didn't want to go lay hands on Saul because he knew that Saul persecuted Christians, and had even come to Damascus for that very purpose (vv. 13–14). This shows that Saul was known to Christians throughout the region as a persecutor of the church.

4. Immediately after his conversion, Saul began proclaiming boldly that Jesus is the Christ (v. 22) and the Son of God (v. 20). He grew in spiritual strength (v. 22) and had fellowship with the disciples whom he had come to persecute (v. 19)!

5. Before Saul encountered Jesus on the road to Damascus, he did not believe that Jesus was the Messiah, and he certainly did not believe that he was God's Son. But when Jesus confronted Saul on the road to Damascus, Saul came to understand that Jesus truly is Israel's Messiah (v. 22), that he is the divine Son of God (v. 20), and that he is therefore the Lord who has authority over all.

6. Saul's conversion is similar to all Christians' in that we are converted only by a sovereign, miraculous act of God, of which this is an especially vivid example. Saul's conversion is also similar to all Christians' in that all those who have been truly converted will bear real spiritual fruit. Their lives will change in demonstrable, evident ways, just as Saul's did.

7. Saul's conversion is different from other Christians' conversions in that:

- Christ appeared to Saul personally, which is totally unique.
- Saul was specifically commissioned to be an apostle, which, again, is unique (vv. 15–16).
- Saul immediately began to publicly preach, which is rare to say the least.
- No human being preached the gospel to him, since Jesus's personal appearance to him made it unnecessary. Today, the only way for someone to be converted is to hear the gospel preached.

8. Paul says that he was formerly a blasphemer, persecutor, and insolent opponent (v. 13). He says that he acted in ignorance and unbelief (v. 13). He calls himself the foremost of sinners (v. 15).

9. Paul received *mercy* from Christ (v. 13).

10. The trustworthy saying Paul gives us is that Christ Jesus came into the world to save sinners. Paul says that this message deserves full acceptance; that is, all people should believe it (v. 15).

11. Paul received mercy in order to be an example of Christ's perfect patience toward those who were to believe in Christ after him (v. 16).

12. The fact that Paul is an example of those who were to believe means that he stands as a model, a paradigm, of a sinner who received grace and mercy from Christ. If Paul, a violent, insolent, blaspheming persecutor of the church, can be saved by God's grace, then surely anyone who turns from their sin and trusts in Christ can be saved. This teaches us that *anyone* can experience the real change that comes through faith in Christ.

13. Paul says that some of us Christians were sexually immoral, idolaters, adulterers, or men who practice homosexuality, thieves, greedy, drunkards, and revilers. We were unrighteous people who were not going to inherit the kingdom of God (vv. 9–11).

14. Paul says that we were washed, we were sanctified, we were justified in the name of the Lord Jesus Christ (v. 11). This means that through Christ our sins were forgiven and we were counted righteous in God's sight ("justified"). And we were cleansed from our impure actions ("washed") and given new, holy natures by God ("sanctified"). In other words, our status before God and our very natures have been totally transformed. We who are Christians have been changed in the most radical ways imaginable.

15. An appropriate response would be something like, "It's true that *by our own power* we can't fundamentally change because all people are enslaved to sin. But through the gospel, God can work deep, lasting, supernatural change in people. We see this in Scripture, and we see this in the lives of those who believe in Christ today."

16. Answers will vary.

TEACHER'S NOTES FOR WEEK 3

DIGGING IN

1. Nicodemus says that he knows Jesus is a teacher from God, because no one could do the things Jesus does unless God is with him (v. 2).

2. In response, Jesus tells Nicodemus that he must be born again.

3. On one level, Nicodemus seems to understand what Jesus is saying, in that he understands that Jesus is calling for a total transformation that's akin to what happens at physical birth. But he also seems to think that what Jesus is saying is impossible. When Nicodemus asks, "How can a man be born when he is old? Can he enter a second time into his mother's womb and be born?" he probably is not seriously asking whether or not a man can reenter his mother's womb. Rather, he's expressing his incredulity at the kind of change Jesus is demanding. So in the end, whatever Nicodemus understood of what Jesus was saying, he fundamentally missed the point because he thought such change was impossible.

4. In light of Ezekiel 36:24–28, it seems that being born of water and the Spirit simply means that we're born by the Holy Spirit whom God gives, who then indwells us and cleanses us from sin. That's what the "water" imagery in the Ezekiel passage means, and it seems that Jesus is deliberately picking up the imagery of this passage in his statement about being born of water and the Spirit.

5. People who are born of the Spirit are like the wind and its effects in that the wind seems to act mysteriously, as if it has a mind of its own, yet you can tell its presence by its effects. In a similar way, the Holy Spirit gives people the new birth according to his own sovereign will. You can't see the Holy Spirit, but you can tell his presence by his effects. The point of Jesus's comparison is that the new birth is something that God sovereignly works in us, not that we initiate and accomplish ourselves.

6. Again, it seems that on one level Nicodemus understands what Jesus is calling for, but on another level he fails to grasp what Jesus is saying. We see this in his response: "How can these things be?" (v. 9).

7. Jesus responds to Nicodemus by chastising him for his ignorance: he should have known these things from studying Scripture (v. 10). Further, Jesus rebukes him for not receiving Jesus's testimony (v. 11). And Jesus warns him that he will not be able to receive "heavenly things" (v. 12).

8. Jesus says that he must be lifted up (namely, by dying on a cross) in order that whoever believes in him may have eternal life (vv. 14–15).

9. An appropriate summary would be something like: Jesus teaches that in order to enter God's kingdom a person must be born again (v. 3). That is, God the Holy Spirit must give a person new life, cleansing him from sin (v. 5) and enabling him to come to faith in Christ (v. 15) and receive God's truth.

10. This change comes about through the gracious, sovereign action of God alone, not through our efforts.

11–12. Answers will vary.

TEACHER'S NOTES FOR WEEK 4

DIGGING IN

1. In this passage Peter exhorts us to love one another earnestly from a pure heart (v. 22).

2. Peter exhorts us to do this on the basis of our having cleansed our souls by our obedience to the truth (v. 22) and our having been born again (v. 23).

3. We have been born again through the living and abiding Word of God (v. 23). That is, we have been born again through hearing God's Word and God causing that Word to effectually work in our hearts to bring us to repent of our sins and trust in Christ.

4. That the Word of God is imperishable seed means that it never fails. It is always true. It is always powerful to accomplish God's purposes. That we have been born again through this imperishable seed means that the life it gives us is eternal life (see also 1 Pet. 1:3–5).

5. The Word of God that gives us the new birth is the gospel, the good news about what God has done to save sinners through the death and resurrection of Jesus Christ.

6. Paul says that before we were converted, we 1) were dead in our trespasses and sins, which characterized our entire way of life; 2) lived according to the course of this world; 3) followed the prince of the power of the air (that is, Satan), and the spirit that is at work among all those who disobey God; 4) lived in the passions of our flesh, carrying out the desires of our sinful nature and our minds; and 5) were by nature "children of wrath," that is, subject to God's wrath because we are sinners by nature. This is a description of total spiritual death, degradation, and alienation from God.

7. What brought about such radical change in our lives is that God raised us from spiritual death and united us to Christ. From the rest of the New Testament, including the passage we just considered in 1 Peter, we know that this happened when God graciously enabled us to repent of our sins and accept the gospel message that was preached to us (see also Eph. 1:13–14).

8. God saved us, gave us new life, and raised us up with Christ because he is rich in mercy and he has great love toward us—a love he demonstrated to us even when we were dead in our transgressions. This teaches us that God is a God of grace, that he does not treat us as our sins deserve, but gives those who believe in Christ what we do not deserve, namely, salvation from sin

and eternal life with him. To learn more about God's love for us despite our sin, read Romans 5:6–11.

9. The results of conversion this passage describes are: 1) we're united to Christ (v. 5); 2) we're made alive with Christ (v. 5); 3) we're raised up and seated in the heavenly places with Christ (v. 6); 4) we're promised that God will eternally show the riches of his grace in kindness to us in Christ (v. 7); and 5) we begin to walk in the good works which God has prepared in advance for us (v. 10).

10. First, Paul clearly teaches that we are not saved by our good works, but by God's grace alone (vv. 8–9). Our good works are not the source of our salvation; rather, God's free grace, mercy, and love are the source of our salvation, which we receive by God's grace, through faith (v. 8). Yet if God has truly saved us, we will grow in doing good works that genuinely please God, which demonstrates the genuineness of our faith. As Paul says, "For we are his workmanship, created in Christ Jesus for good works, which God prepared beforehand, that we should walk in them" (v. 10).

11. Answers will vary, but here are some suggestions:

- It's important for a local church to teach on how conversion happens so that people will be converted, so that they will be able to have an accurate knowledge of whether they've been converted, so that church members will evangelize biblically, and more.
- Some results of good teaching on the topic would be the things mentioned above. Some results of bad teaching would include members who think they're converted but are not, members who use unbiblical techniques in evangelism in order to try to force "decisions," and so on.

12. Answers will vary, but some possibilities include the style of the preacher's clothes, the style of music, the look of the building, the lighting, the humor in the sermon, our intelligence, and so many other things. None of these things are wrong to be mindful of. Still, we must always remember that a person can only be "born again . . . through the living and abiding word of God."

13. Answers will vary, but here are some suggestions:

a) Reflecting on God's work of conversion should remind us that he is the one who converts people. This should encourage us to evangelize. It should also encourage us to keep evangelizing even when we don't see immediate fruit, since we know that God is powerful to save. It should also cause us to evangelize in a way that calls people to repent and trust in Christ, yet recognizes that that decision is not in *our* power to bring about.

b) Reflecting on the fact that we were dead in sins and God raised us to life should make us humble. The spiritual life we now have is a result of God's gracious work. Thus, we should respond to criticism humbly and appreciatively, recognizing that we are not the source of our growth in godliness and that we need all the help we can get.

c) Reflecting on God's work of conversion should prompt us to pray that our unsaved family and friends would be converted. It should give us hope and perseverance in praying this. It should also encourage us to pray for all sorts of ways we and others need to grow in godliness, since the God who is able to raise us from spiritual death is also able to bring change in our lives.

d) The fact that we were all dead in sin and have been made alive by God should cause us to cultivate and cherish a profound unity with fellow church members. It should cause us to bear patiently with the sins and failures of our brothers and sisters, since we know that their deepest, God-given desire is to honor and obey him. And so on.

TEACHER'S NOTES FOR WEEK 5

DIGGING IN

1. In Christ, God has made us his children. This shows that God is richly loving toward us, and that he is gracious and merciful and generous.

2. When John says "what we will be has not yet appeared," he means that when Jesus comes, we will be made perfectly holy as Jesus is holy. Yet all throughout the present life, we still struggle against sin, because we have not yet been made perfect.

3. John says that everyone who hopes in Jesus purifies himself, as he is pure. We do this because of the hope we have of one day being made perfectly pure by God himself.

Practically speaking, we do this by:

- Confessing sin
- Turning from sin
- Seeking to grow in holiness through the means God has provided:
  - Weekly assembling with his people to encourage each other, hear God's Word preached, and worship God
  - Praying to God: confessing our sins, praising him, and asking for what we need
- Reading and meditating on God's Word, and so on.

4. Jesus "appeared," that is, came to earth, to take away sins and to destroy the works of the Devil (vv. 5, 8).

5. According to John, people who habitually practice sin:

   a) Also practice *lawlessness* (v. 4).
   b) Have neither *seen* nor *known* Jesus (v. 6).
   c) Are of *the Devil* (v. 8).
   d) Are not *of God* (v. 10).

6. It seems that John warns his readers in this way because there are people who were teaching that you could be a Christian and continue to live a life of sin.

7. According to John, everyone who is truly born again:

   a) *Purifies* himself (v. 3).

b) Doesn't *keep on sinning* (v. 6).

c) Practices *righteousness* (v. 7).

d) Does not and cannot *make a practice* of sinning (v. 9).

8. No one who is born of God keeps on sinning because God's seed abides in him, since he has been born of God (v. 9). This means that in the new birth, God imparts a new, supernatural life to us, which will inevitably lead to our living a new and holy life. Because we have a new nature which delights to do God's will, we simply cannot go on living as we did before.

9. In saying all this, John is clearly *not* teaching that Christians are perfect and never sin. In fact, in 1 John 1:8–9, he says "If we say we have no sin, we deceive ourselves, and the truth is not in us. If we confess our sins, he is faithful and just to forgive us our sins and to cleanse us from all unrighteousness." And again, in 1 John 2:1–2 John writes, "My little children, I am writing these things to you so that you may not sin. But if anyone does sin, we have an advocate with the Father, Jesus Christ the righteous. He is the propitiation for our sins, and not for ours only but also for the sins of the whole world."

10. Some ways that churches obscure or contradict this truth include:

a) In their preaching, pastors can make it seem as if a simple decision that doesn't change a single thing in a person's life is actually real conversion. In other words, they ignore the Bible's teaching that genuine conversion produces love for the saints.

b) Churches can accept people into membership without even stopping to consider whether a person's life demonstrates fruit of conversion.

c) The comment on membership above also applies to baptism. Also, churches can obscure the truth that conversion leads to love for others by allowing people who are living in flagrant sin to partake of the Lord's Supper.

d) In their small groups and other contexts for fellowship, churches can simply settle for superficial niceness rather than cultivating genuine, sacrificial love among members. They can also treat these contexts as cliques or clubs, rather than seeking to embody the diversity of the body of Christ by loving and welcoming all different kinds of people.

11. Some ways that churches display and recognize this truth include:

a) Preaching and teaching that love for fellow Christians is a necessary fruit of conversion.

b) Being careful to admit into membership only people who clearly embrace the Christian faith, and whose lives show some evidence of love for God and others.

c) See above. Also by practicing church discipline.

d) Using small groups and other contexts for fellowship to cultivate and demonstrate real love within the body of Christ. Ways to do this include transparently discussing sins and struggles, serving each other in practical ways, having a gracious, open spirit toward people who are different than oneself, and so on.

12. Answers will vary.

TEACHER'S NOTES FOR WEEK 6

DIGGING IN

1. In this passage, the only thing John explicitly commands us to do is love one another (vv. 7, 11, 21). Interestingly, though, he commands us to do this three times, underscoring how crucial it is for Christians to love each other.

2. John says that those who love one another are born of God and know God (v. 7), they have God abiding in them and God's love abiding in them (v. 12), and they abide in God (v. 16).

3. John says that those who do not love one another do not know God (v. 8) and cannot love God (v. 20).

4. God has shown his love for us by sending his Son into the world to be the propitiation for our sins, becoming our Savior, so that we might live through him (vv. 9–10, 14). "Propitiation" means "a sacrifice which turns away God's wrath." In his death on the cross, Jesus paid the penalty our sins deserved, satisfying God's just wrath against us.

5. John teaches that we should love each other because:

- Love is from God, and whoever loves has been born of God (v. 7). In other words, we should love because, as Christians, it's our nature to love.
- God has loved us richly in sending Christ to be our Savior (v. 11).
- God has loved us first (v. 19).
- God commands us to love each other (v. 21).

6. John teaches that when we love each other:

- God abides, that is, dwells, in us and his love is perfected in us (v. 12).
- Not only does God abide in us, but we abide in him (v. 16).
- Love is perfected in us, which casts out fear and gives us confidence for the day of judgment (vv. 17–18).

7. This passage teaches that someone does not love God if they do not love their fellow Christians. John says, "If anyone says, 'I love God,' and hates his brother, he is a liar; for he who does not love his brother whom he has seen cannot love God whom he has not seen" (v. 20).

8. Cain killed Abel because Abel's deeds were righteous and his own deeds were wicked. As John Piper puts it,

> He killed him because the contrast between Abel's goodness and Cain's evil made Cain angry. It made him feel guilty. Abel didn't have to say anything; Abel's goodness was a constant reminder to Cain that he was evil. And instead of dealing with his own evil by repentance and change, he got rid of Abel. If you don't like what you see in the mirror, shoot the mirror.[1]

This teaches us that sin hates to be exposed by someone else's righteousness.

9. The negative example of Cain teaches us that we should love others by celebrating their spiritual maturity and growth. We should give thanks to God for the growth we see in others. We should celebrate and rejoice when others walk faithfully with the Lord. And, instead of resenting others' holiness because of how it exposes our sins, we should repent of those sins and thank God for the convicting work of his Holy Spirit.

10. John says that we should lay down our lives for our brothers because Jesus laid down his life for us (v. 16).

11. John says that we are to love one another in deed and in truth, not merely in word and talk (v. 18). The test he gives for our love is whether we are willing to provide for other Christians' material needs (v. 17).

12–13. Answers will vary.

---

[1] John Piper, *Finally Alive* (Fearns, UK: Christian Focus, 2009), 158.

TEACHER'S NOTES FOR WEEK 7

DIGGING IN

1. Peter's hearers experienced conviction of sin as they listened to his address (v. 37). As Peter proclaimed the truth about Christ, they became convinced of their guilt before God and their need for salvation. They responded by asking the apostles, "Brothers, what shall we do?" (v. 37).

2. Peter told his hearers to repent, to be baptized, and to save themselves from the present wicked generation (vv. 38, 40). Implicit in all three things is that they must believe in Jesus Christ. It's clear that this is the case because in verse 44, all those who responded to Peter's message are referred to as those who believed.

3. Peter says that God's promise "is for you and for your children and for all who are far off, everyone whom the Lord our God calls to himself" (Acts 2:39). This means that conversion is possible for all, that it's not limited to any single group of people. It also teaches that conversion is God's work, that it comes about when God powerfully and effectually calls people to himself through the gospel.

4. "There were added that day about three thousand souls" (Acts 2:41) means that on that day, three thousand people repented of their sins, put their trust in Christ, were baptized, and were joined to the church. What were they added to? They were added to the church in Jerusalem, the body of people who believed that Jesus is the Messiah and that he rose from the dead. And as we'll see, their joining the church was no mere formality. It radically impacted every aspect of their lives.

5. As a unified body, these new believers devoted themselves to:

- "The apostles' teaching" (v. 42). They diligently sought to learn all they could from those who were authoritative eyewitnesses of the resurrection of Jesus.
- "The fellowship" (v. 42). The Greek word *koinonia*, here translated "fellowship," refers to the believers' common life together. As John Stott has put it, what the believers shared *in* together was fellowship with God the Father, Son, and Holy Spirit. What the believers shared *out* together was their time, their hospitality, and their possessions, living in close fellowship with each other.[1]

---

[1] John R. W. Stott, *The Message of Acts* (Downers Grove, IL: InterVarsity, 1994), 83.

- "The breaking of bread" (v. 42). This probably refers to the early believers' practice of regularly eating together. Their meals were characterized by joy, praise toward God, and heartfelt generosity (v. 46).
- "The prayers" (v. 42). This probably refers to their participation in set times of prayer at the temple. But given that we also know that they praised God together when they ate, it seems that prayer was common in all of their corporate activities.

6. These new believers shared all of their possessions with each other (v. 44), and they even sold their possessions to give to those who had need (v. 45). This shows us that their love for God manifested itself in love for their fellow Christians. First John 3:16–18 teaches us that this is a mark of all genuine Christians.

7. Verses 46 and 47 tell us that day by day, the believers attended the temple together and shared meals together in their homes with joy and gladness, praising God and having favor with all the people.

8. Verse 47 teaches us that day by day, the Lord added more and more believers to the church. This teaches us that these Christians were regularly sharing the gospel with those around them, and that God was blessing their efforts by bringing many to faith in Christ.

9. Answers will vary.

10. Churches might unwittingly allow unconverted persons into membership by simply allowing people to join without ever asking them questions about their understanding of the gospel, how they came to believe in Christ, and what their lives have been like since then. In other words, churches may unwittingly allow unconverted people into membership by simply failing to stop and see whether people manifest any fruits of conversion.

11. a) Churches can help ensure that those who join are truly converted by asking applicants for membership to explain their understanding of the gospel, how they became Christians, and how their lives have changed since then in order to become members of the church. b) Churches can help ensure that all those who are converted join and plant their lives in a church by constantly teaching on and highlighting church membership. They can also make membership more meaningful by restricting activities such as leading in the church's public services and small groups to those who have committed to the church through membership.

12. Answers will vary.

PERSONAL NOTES

PERSONAL NOTES

9Marks

Building Healthy Churches

9Marks exists to equip church leaders with a biblical vision and practical resources for displaying God's glory to the nations through healthy churches.

To that end, we want to see churches characterized by these nine marks of health:

1   Expositional Preaching
2   Biblical Theology
3   A Biblical Understanding of the Gospel
4   A Biblical Understanding of Conversion
5   A Biblical Understanding of Evangelism
6   Biblical Church Membership
7   Biblical Church Discipline
8   Biblical Discipleship
9   Biblical Church Leadership

**Find all our Crossway titles
and other resources at
www.9Marks.org**

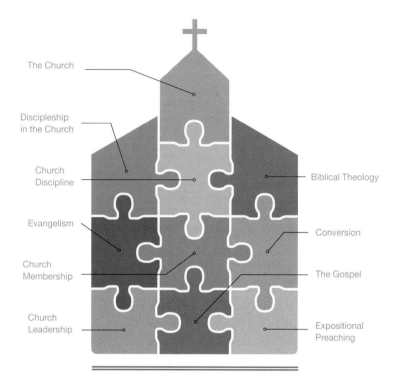

The Church

Discipleship in the Church

Church Discipline

Evangelism

Church Membership

Church Leadership

Biblical Theology

Conversion

The Gospel

Expositional Preaching

Be sure to check out the rest of the
9MARKS HEALTHY CHURCH STUDY GUIDE SERIES

This series covers the nine distinctives of a healthy church as originally laid out in *Nine Marks of a Healthy Church* by Mark Dever. Each book explores the biblical foundations of key aspects of the church, helping Christians to live out those realities as members of a local body. A perfect resource for use in Sunday school, church-wide studies, or small group contexts.